GRAND TOUR

GRAND TOUR

COLLECTED LYRICS BY

ROD McKUEN

STANYAN BOOKS

RANDOM HOUSE

A Stanyan Book
Published by Stanyan Books,
8721 Sunset Blvd., Suite C
Hollywood, California 90069
and by Random House, Inc.
201 East 50th Street
New York, N.Y. 10022

Library of Congress Catalog
Card Number: 72-81612

ISBN: 0-394-48214-x

Printed in U.S.A.

Designed by Hy Fujita

**For J. and Wade
and the memory of Shep**

INTRODUCTION

In the last two years Rod McKuen has spent the major part of his time traveling and giving concerts in Canada, England, Holland, France, Germany, Austria, Ireland, Australia and New Zealand—and in America, every state but ten. During that time he has appeared before an estimated two million people, a record probably unmatched by anyone in the popular or classical field. In 1972 alone he gave more than 180 concerts and lectures.

In addition, during that year he found time to compose two new major classical works, score a film, complete innumerable songs and at least one new book, while working for meaningful legislation on behalf of domestic animals as well as wildlife.

According to Cleveland Amory of *The Saturday Review*, "Rod McKuen is the country's number one, one-man communications empire." Nowhere is 'communication' more evident than at a Rod McKuen concert. There is a one-to-one feeling that comes across no matter what the age group or nationality, and a mutual understanding between artist and audience that is the same whether he is performing for 1500 or 30,000.

Several of Rod's concerts have been recorded in the past two years, most notably The Amsterdam Concert (a double album made during a remarkable performance he gave at The Concertgebouw in the fall of 1971.) In addition, three albums—a two-record set entitled *Grand Tour*, and *Grand Tour Vol. 3*, made up of performances in New York, Santa Monica, London and Denver, Colorado—were released throughout the world to wide critical acclaim and have become an indispensable part of anyone's Rod McKuen collection.

The lyrics in this book have been selected from those recordings, and the photographs chosen by Hy Fujita from the hundreds taken on the tour by Wayne Massie, David Nutter and Mr. Fujita himself.

This book has been designed as a visual companion to a series of recordings that continue to form an almost documentary study of a man who has become an important spokesman for all of us . . . or as *The New York Times* sums it up, "Few entertainers deserve or earn the word 'star' or 'legend'— Rod McKuen is one of those select few. Every concert is better than the last."

— Willard Andlen

CONTENTS

APRIL PEOPLE

April, April,
laugh your happy laughter
but a moment after
cry your gentle tears.

April people try to smile
even when they're sad
'cause they know
behind the rainbow
things can't be that bad.

April people all are lonely
that's the general rule
and more than once a lonely heart
has made an April fool.

Born in April, sad of heart,
you're a lonesome child,
but you could make the sun shine
with even half a smile.

April people live for love
nothing else will do.
So come along and take my hand,
I was born in April, too.

FRIENDLY SOUNDS

Hello my friend,
my funny friend,
why are you lookin' so down?
Make me a laugh,
well maybe half
and I'll show you
all my friendly sounds.
Listen and hear
inside your ear
all kinds of pretty things
talkin' to you.

Listen to the rain
on the windowpane,
listen to the cricket
on the hearth,
and if you should hear
thunder in your ear
it's just the friendly sounding
of your heart.

20

I know you cry.
Well so do I,
but when I really get low
I think about
the distance to doubt
and find it's too far to go.
So dry your eyes,
pick up your pride.
Oh yes, my weepy friend,
I'm talkin' to you.

Listen to the rain
on the windowpane,
listen to the cricket
on the hearth,
and if you should hear
thunder in your ear
it's just the friendly sounding
of your heart.

MY MARY

For Mary Travers

She's dancin' down in Denver, my Mary,
she's singin' in Chicago
and flingin' back her hair
and tomorrow she'll be wingin' home
through the early winter.
Tomorrow she'll be miles and smiles away,
    my Mary,
tomorrow she'll be miles and smiles away.

She's roarin' up at Red Rocks, my Mary,
she's blinkin' at the spotlight
and thinkin' up a prayer,
tomorrow she'll be winkin'
at the New York City skyline.
Tomorrow she'll be tears and years away,
    my Mary,
tomorrow she'll be tears and years away.

She's sighted in the window now by Erika
and Jerry sees her comin' up the stair
and the best that I can wish for her
is all the love she gave me
on half-a-dozen English afternoons.

I'm sittin' and rememberin' my Mary,
I'm following her thoughts,
swallowing with care.
Tomorrow while I'm wallowing
in California sunshine
my Mary will be days and ways away,
    my Mary,
my Mary will be days and ways away.

And the best that I can wish for her
is all the love she gave me
on half-a-dozen English afternoons.

SO MANY OTHERS

For Liesbeth List

Comfort me with apples
torture me with tears
make up for the lonely days
and all the lonesome years.
Place your little fingers
here within my hand,
there've been so many others
who didn't understand.

Bring me pretty marbles
the best that you can find,
sing to me of rivers
it helps to ease my mind.
Talk me pretty love words
and I will do the same,
there've been so many others
who didn't ask my name.
They'd look at me and wonder
what is he thinking of
when all I ever wanted
was lullabies and love.

Tell me that I'm handsome
and lots of other lies,
come along and love me
with little summer sighs.
And even if you leave me
pretend your love is true,
there've been so many others
there might as well be you.

ROUND, ROUND, ROUND

Round, round, round,
we'll watch the world go round
and if your world breaks down
I'll be around.
What we've found
has to be something sound
or like a merry-go-round
it will break down.

I've never loved more
than how I love now
and likely I won't love again.
And so please excuse my enthusiasm
in trying to catch the brass ring.

Round, round, round,
like a top spinning around,
catch every sight and sound
as we go round.

ONE DAY SOON

I may not find the clover
but at least I'll have a try.
And who knows, maybe one day soon
I'll catch the wave and ride
from here to way out yonder
somewhere beyond somewhere
where love's as familiar
as the back of my hand
and safe as breathin' air.

I may not find the rainbow
but at least I'll have a try.
And who knows, maybe one day soon
I'll tell the town goodbye
and start off on my journey
to find what I must find
a place where love's as real as the rain
and not just a word in the mind.

One day soon
I'll walk with the giants up the hill
and love'll come runnin' after me,
it will, it will, it will.

I've seen a hundred sunsets
that crowned a thousand days
and I guess that there must easily be
fifteen hundred ways
to get to where you're goin',
the corner or the moon.
Well I don't know where I'm goin'
but I'll get there one day soon.

EACH OF US ALONE

So many old men sitting in the park
waiting for the dawn to come
and chase away the dark.
But the night never shakes
the stars from out its hair
and the old men just sit there
and sit there and sit there.

So many ladies all in tailored suits,
if they found a man to love
they'd polish up his boots.
But all the men in all the towns
were stolen by some crook
and the ladies just look
and look and look.

Each of us alone, apart,
each of us alone.
Oh the worlds we might have known
if we'd found something to call our own.
A dandelion day, perhaps,
that finally took us home
something that didn't go away
leaving us each alone.

So many young men shouting in the street
calling down the stars
to help them get up on their feet.
But the stars got troubles of their own
without a doubt
and the young men just shout
and shout and shout.

So many little girls chatting in a room
thinking that talk alone
can chase away the gloom.
But all the words in all the world
are whispered on the wind
and the little girls chat,
the young men shout,
the ladies look,
while the old men sit
and sit and sit.

MISTER KELLY
(Kelly and Me)

Hey Mr. Kelly, ain't it a thrill
just to go runnin' down some green hill
rollin' on the green grass, walkin' by the sea.
Caught in the sunshine, Kelly and me
singin' in the sunshine, runnin' by the sea
always together, Kelly and me.

Well you might wonder where Katie's gone
chasin' the shadows down on the dawn
barkin' at strangers she'll never see.
I'll bet she remembers Kelly and me
singin' in the sunshine, runnin' by the sea,
always together, Kelly and me.

Hey Mr. Kelly, when we grow old
who'll give us comfort and care from the cold?
What does it matter, long as we're free
and always together, Kelly and me
runnin' on the green grass, walkin' by the sea
barkin' at butterflies, Kelly and me.

SONG FROM THE EARTH

One drop of rain
cannot fill a fountain,
one grain of sand
doesn't make a mountain.
And a handful of dirt
is just about all we're worth
in the eyes of the man
who made us all from the earth.

Those who go alone
those who go together
those who give the world its trouble
those who make it better,
we're all on our way to dust
from the day of our birth.

From the ground we've come
and we're all going back to earth,
so stay for a while with me
walk another mile with me ,
live another day for what it's worth.
Tomorrow and tomorrow and tomorrow
we'll go back to the earth.

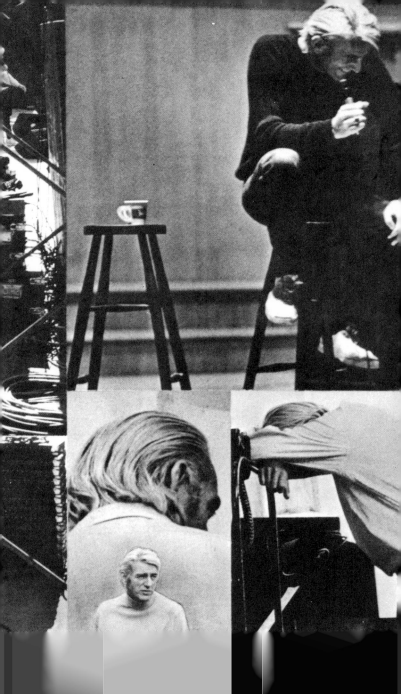

FIVE FOR THE FUN OF IT
(A Cycle of Not-So-Greatest Hits)

1. The Hart

The hart he loves the high road
the hare he loves the hill
I love the pretty girls
all against their will.

2. The Tasmanian Devil Song

Young men go courtin'
they tell ladies lies
and if one resists 'em
they muffle her cries.

3. Knicker Kicker

She comes from a line of martyrs
the pills she takes are Carters'
she uses barbed wire for garters.
You ought to see the scars on my hand.

4. The Spider

Little spider on the wall
you ain't got no hair at all
you ain't got no comb
to comb your hair.
What do you care?
You ain't got no hair.

5. Sing Out, Louise

When Aunt Louise fell off the boat
and couldn't swim and wouldn't float
and young Miranda sat and smiled
I almost could have slapped the child.

THE SUMMER'S LONG

A friend lay dying
and I could have said,
raise your head a little
and I'll try to show you Spain.
But he slipped away
and I'll never have the chance again.
And the summer's long, long, long,
and the summer's long.

There was a man so hungry
and I could have given him bread,
bread costs very little
it's much cheaper than the rain.
But he went away
and I'll never have the chance again.
And the summer's long, long, long,
and the summer's long.

There was a girl who loved me
and I could have held her head
against my chest
and helped to ease her pain.
But she's gone away
and I'll never have the chance again.
And the summer's long, long, long,
and the summer's long.

There is a world so needy
but we treat it like it's dead,
I don't know what
we all expect to gain.
One day it will be gone
and we'll never have the chance again.
And the summer's long, long, long,
and the summer's long.

WITHOUT A WORRY IN THE WORLD

You all have seen the vagabond
as he went singin' in the dawn
without a worry in the world.
I've never known a gypsy who
could be a gypsy through and through
and have a worry in the world.
All merry men are minstrels then
who keep their troubles locked inside,
and don't inflict them on the world.
Isn't there something to be said
for leavin' your troubles in your head
never takin' them to the world?

The sailor cruising in the town
is not afraid to be a clown
without a worry in the world.
No cowboy with an ounce of pride
will mount his horse and ride
and have a worry in the world.
All merry men are minstrels then
who keep their troubles locked inside,
and don't inflict them on the world.
Isn't there something to be said
for leavin' your troubles home in bed,
never takin' them to the world?

If I must love then let me love
as though I've never loved before
without a worry in the world.
And when I go then let me go
and only gently close the door
without a worry in the world.
For I'm a man, a minstrel man
who keeps his troubles locked inside.
I won't inflict them on the world,
and isn't there something to be said
for having had some love instead
or never having any in the world?

Without a worry in the world
without a worry in the world,
yes, I've got troubles of my own
but I can take them all alone,
I won't inflict them on the world.

PASTURES GREEN

Each man must find a pasture green
somewhere beyond the western wind,
out where a man can hear
freedom singin' in his ear,
where love, like lightning, touches him.

Some men were born to live each day
fenced in by pavements cold and gray,
but some men can never wait,
locked outside freedom's gate,
they need to find a pasture green.

Tied by the silver thread of time
love comes to each and every man.
And love, when it comes to you
always seems as fresh and new
as God's own wondrous pastures green.
Come, we'll go down through pastures green.

I know each hill
is high and wide
but green pastures fill
the other side
and so I'll travel each trail
and find each stream
and lie down in peace
in a pasture cool and green.

Rod Mc Kuen wears jeans by AMCO of Australia

About The Author

ROD McKUEN was born in Oakland, California, and grew up in California, Nevada, Washington and Oregon. In less than five years his books of poetry have sold over seven million copies in hardcover, making him the best selling and most widely read poet of all time.

His songs and poetry have been translated into Spanish, French, Dutch, German, Russian, Czechoslovakian, Japanese, Chinese, Norwegian and other languages.

His film music has twice been nominated for Motion Picture Academy Awards. His songs have sold over 100 million records and his classical music, including his 1st and 2nd symphonies and his concertos for guitar and harpsichord are performed by leading orchestras throughout Europe.

Despite travelling extensively in Europe and America as both concert artist and writer, the author manages to spend time at home in California in a rambling Spanish house with a menagerie of Old English sheep dogs and five cats. He likes outdoor sports and driving. His latest book of poetry, AND TO EACH SEASON, will be published in the fall of 1972.